Water is a solid, liquid and gas

Anne Dibben

This book is an introduction to the science of water.

You will need to read chapters 1 and 2 before you can fully understand the later points in the book.

Contents

1 What is water?

Water is a clear liquid. It is very important to plants and animals.

▲ All plants and animals need water to live.

Water has no taste or smell. Water looks clear. We can see through it. Water flows from taps. Water falls from clouds and collects in puddles, lakes and the sea.

Plants and animals die if they do not get enough water. People can only survive a few days without water. We can survive much longer without food.

Water is not what it seems. Water is not really colourless. It is very slightly blue. Very deep water is blue.

Water is made up of very tiny droplets of water. Inside each droplet of water there are even smaller water molecules. These molecules are too small for us to see, but they can be seen with very powerful microscopes. Even a tiny raindrop is made of millions of water molecules.

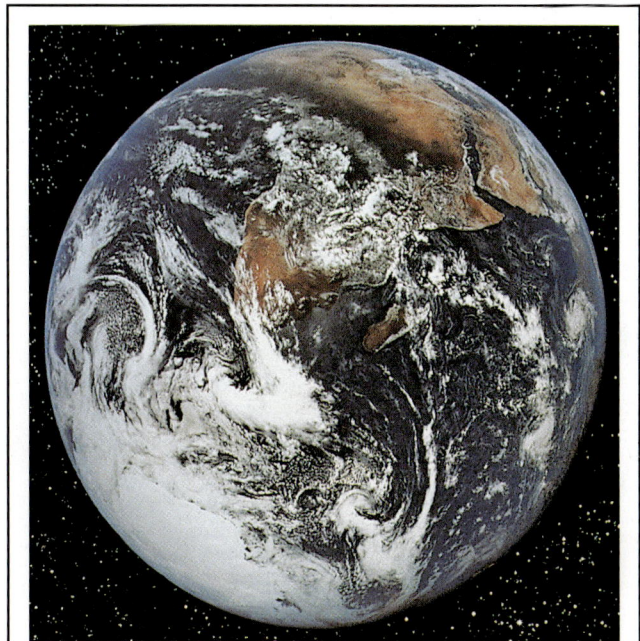

A photograph of Earth taken from space. It shows most of the Earth is covered in water.

3

2 Different forms of water

Most things on Earth are either a solid, a liquid or a gas. Water is very special because it can be a solid, a liquid and a gas.

◀◀ Water is a solid when it freezes into ice.

Water can be found all around us. Sometimes it is a solid, sometimes it is a liquid and sometimes it is a gas.

▲ Water is a liquid when it flows in a river. It is a gas when it is steam.

Water becomes a solid when it freezes. Icebergs are frozen water. Some parts of the world such as the Antarctic are covered in ice all year.

We usually think of water as a liquid. Rain is liquid water. The water flowing in rivers and over waterfalls is liquid water.

Even the air around us contains water. The water in air is called water vapour. Water vapour is like steam, it is water in a gas form.

Water molecules

All water is made up of water molecules. The same water molecules can be used to make ice, liquid water and steam. The reason ice looks different from liquid water is because the molecules in ice behave in a different way to the molecules in liquid water.

Imagine lots of children sitting neatly in rows hardly moving. If the same children start moving, running around and sliding past each other they will appear very different. They are still the same children but they are behaving differently.

◄◄ The molecules in ice stay in one shape.

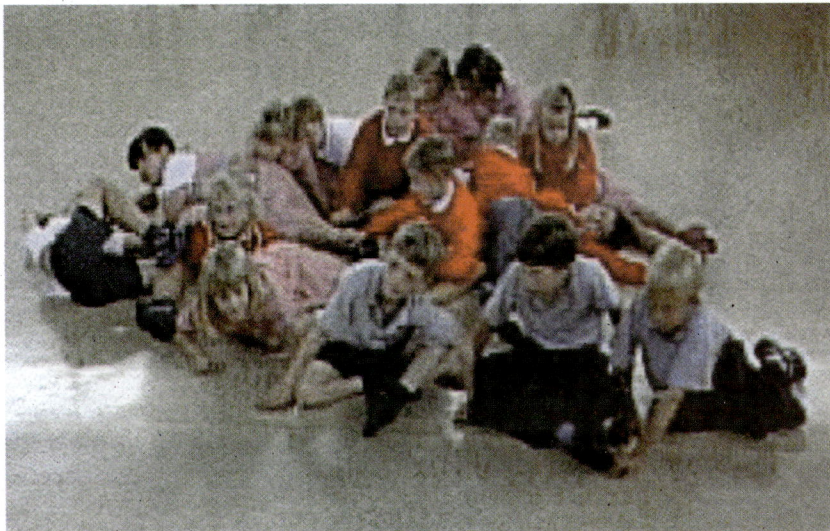

◄◄ The molecules in liquid water are always moving.

3 Water turning to ice (solid)

Water turns to ice when it gets very cold. Ice keeps the same shape if the temperature stays cold. If the temperature gets warmer the ice turns back to water.

Water expands

Water freezes when it changes from liquid water into solid ice. One of the interesting things about water is that it seems to grow when it turns to ice.

If you fill a plastic pot with water and put it in the freezer it will turn to ice. You will see the ice takes up more space than the water. The water has expanded. Water expands when it is frozen. ➤➤

Freezing points

Water has a freezing point of 0° Celsius (0°C). If the temperature goes below this point water freezes. The freezing point is the point at which water becomes ice. This is why if the temperature drops below 0°C puddles freeze over.

If salt is added to water the freezing point changes. When water has salt in it the water needs to be even colder before it will freeze. Sea water needs to be at least 10°C colder than 0°C to change to ice. The freezing point of sea water is −10°C.

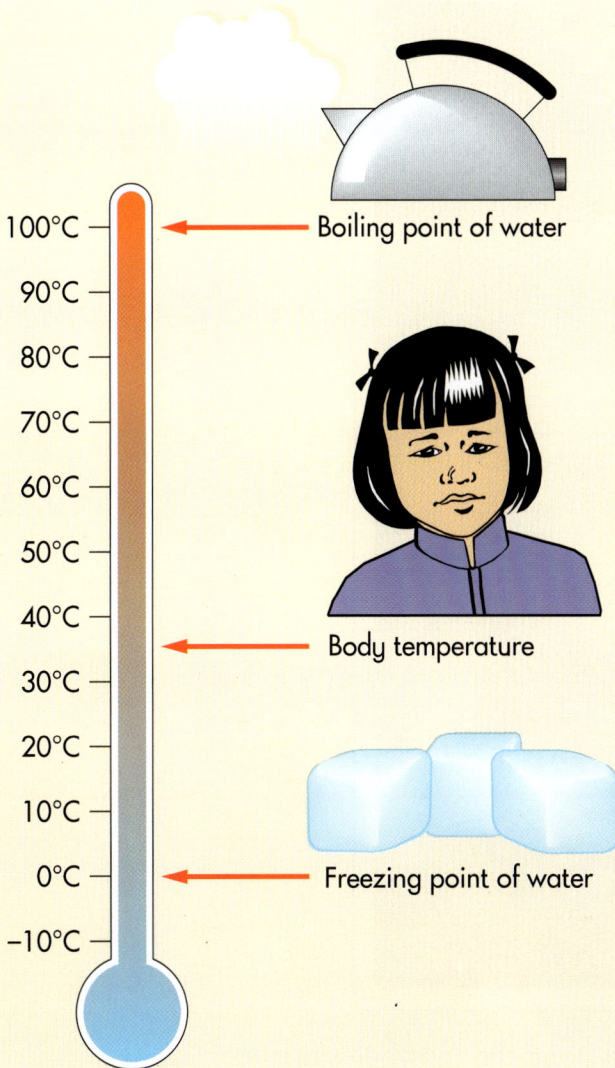

100°C	Boiling point of water
90°C	
80°C	
70°C	
60°C	
50°C	
40°C	
30°C	Body temperature
20°C	
10°C	
0°C	Freezing point of water
−10°C	

A thermometer measures temperature.

4 Ice turning to water (liquid)

The water in ice melts when it gets warmer. Ice always melts when it is pressed. If you press an ice cube with a spoon it will start to melt.

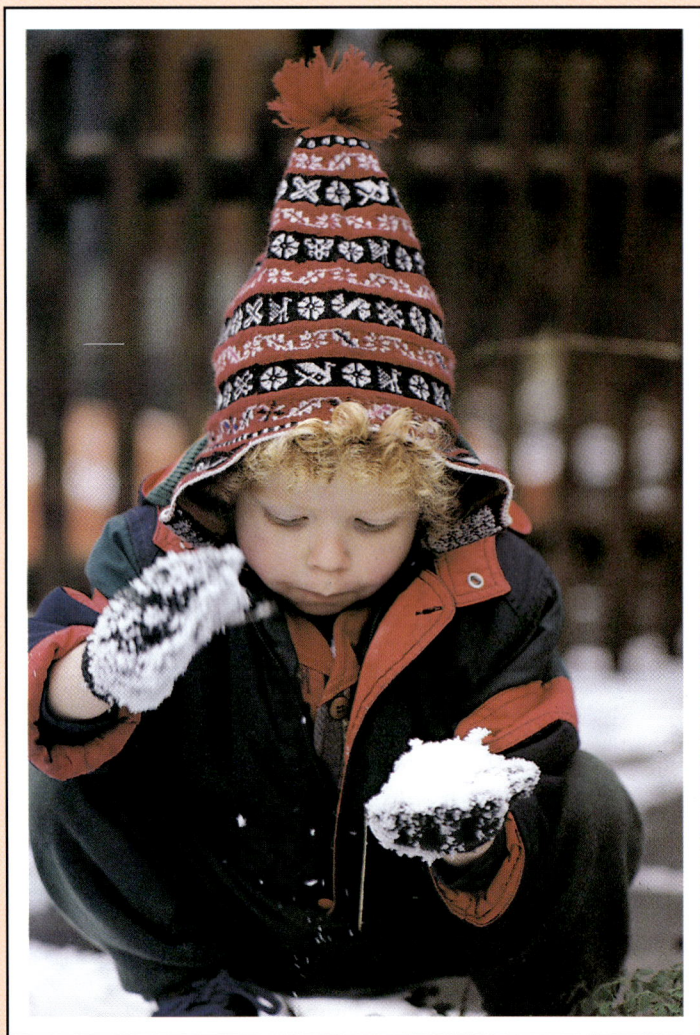

When you hold a snowball in your hand the snowball starts to melt. The heat from your hand warms the ice so it starts to melt. Your hand feels cold because the heat from your hand has been used to melt the snow.

Melting ice using pressure

Ice is very unusual because it changes from a solid (ice) to a liquid (water) when it is pressed or warmed. Even if it is below freezing point you can make ice melt by pressing it. If you walk on ice your feet press on the ice. Where your feet press on the ice it melts. When you lift your foot off, the ice freezes again. Very cold ice needs to be pressed very hard to make it melt. When we press on ice we are using pressure to melt the ice. Pressing on the ice pushes the molecules in the ice closer together. The molecules start to move and slide around each other. The ice is now melting. When the molecules can slide around each other the ice is no longer solid, it is liquid.

This ice is changing into a liquid.

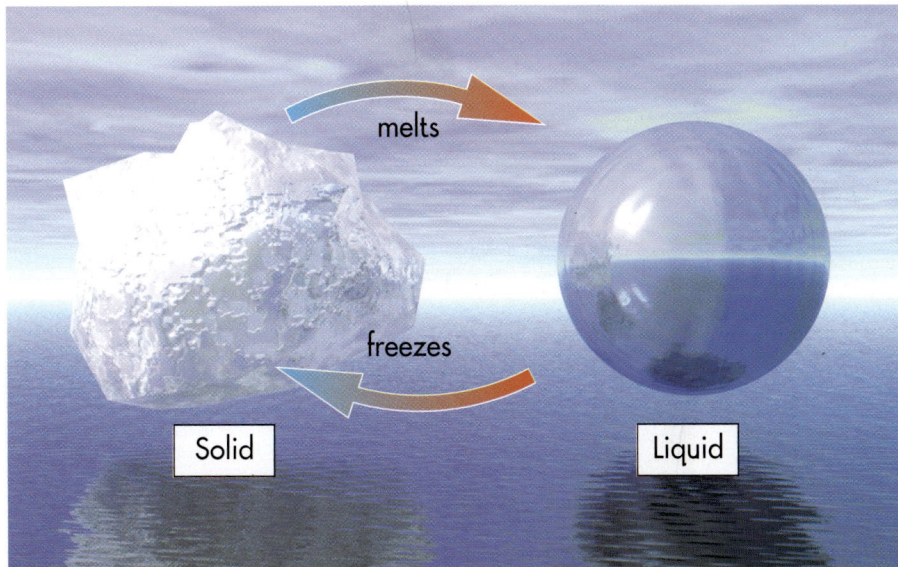

melts

freezes

Solid

Liquid

5 Water turning to water vapour (gas)

Water turns into a gas when the water is hot. This gas is called steam or water vapour.

The hottest temperature liquid water can reach is 100°C. This is the temperature at which water starts to boil. This is called the boiling point. When liquid water boils it turns into a gas. This change from a liquid to a gas is called evaporation. When water evaporates it seems to disappear. This is because you cannot usually see water vapour.

The heat haze is made by water droplets turning into a gas.

Water vapour and molecules

Liquid water evaporates at boiling point because it cannot get any hotter. When water is heated the molecules in the water move faster and faster. At 100°C the molecules are moving so fast they cannot stay together. This works in the same way as when you link hands with lots of people and then start to run around very fast. It is very hard to all stay together, holding hands. The links break and some people will escape from the chain. When water boils the links between the molecules break and some of the molecules escape from the other molecules in the liquid. These molecules create bubbles in the water. The bubbles in the water are steam trapped in the liquid. The bubbles of steam rise to the top of the water and escape into the air. When the steam escapes into the air we call it water vapour.

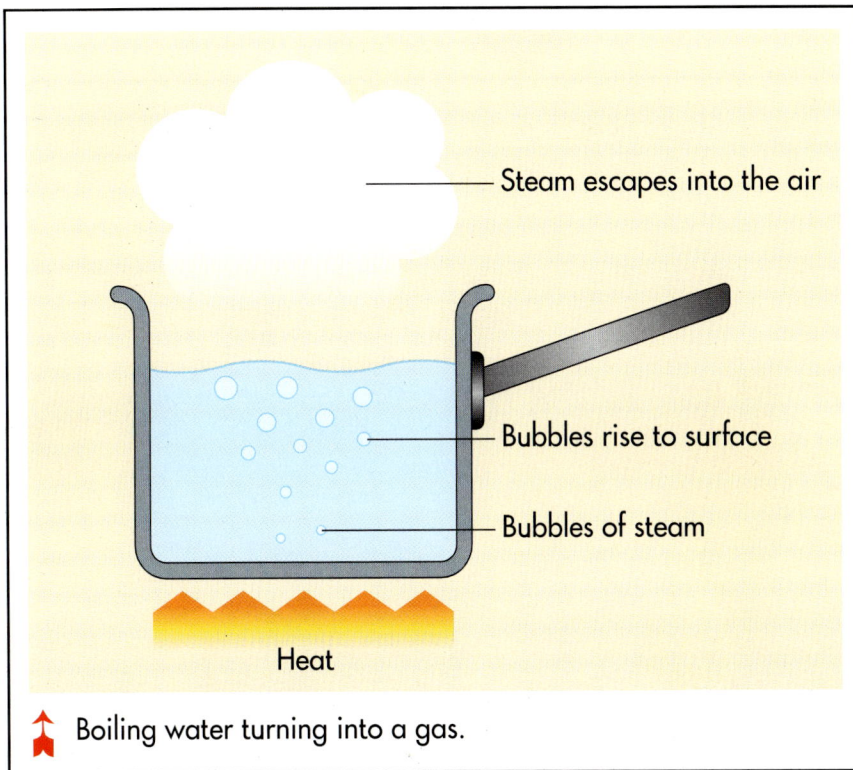

Steam escapes into the air

Bubbles rise to surface

Bubbles of steam

Heat

▲ Boiling water turning into a gas.

How do puddles disappear?

The water at the top of the puddle is warmed by the sun. The water evaporates and rises into the air. Some of the water has changed from a liquid to a gas. The water is now water vapour.

Lots of people think water only turns into a gas when it boils. This is not true. Water does not need to be boiling to turn into a gas. Water can turn into water vapour at almost any temperature. A puddle dries up because the water turns into water vapour which we cannot see and disappears into the air.

6 Water vapour turning to water

Water vapour becomes liquid water when it gets colder.

Water vapour turns into liquid water when it touches something cold. Water vapour rising from a hot drink will become water if it touches a cold window pane.

↥ You see the water vapour turning into liquid on a cold day.

We call the change from vapour to liquid condensation.

Clouds are made when water vapour in the air gets colder and becomes lots of tiny drops of liquid water. These drops are light enough to float in the air. As more water vapour becomes liquid the drops get bigger. When the drops are too heavy to float in the air they fall as rain.

Dew

At night the temperature falls and the air gets cooler. Some of the water vapour in the air touches the cooler grass and other objects and turns into drops of water. These drops of water are called dew. This is why the ground is often wet in the morning even though it has not rained during the night. The point at which the water vapour in the air turns to water is called the dewpoint.

Dew is a drop of water which forms on grass at night.

If it is very cold the water vapour turns into frost at the dewpoint. When water vapour touches a solid object whose temperature is below freezing, the vapour turns into ice.

13

7 Water as a solid – ice

Frozen water is ice. Ice is called a solid because it keeps one shape. Ice will float on water.

Icebergs are large pieces of ice.

Ice is actually made up of lots of tiny ice crystals. Frost and snow are made from a mixture of tiny ice crystals and air.

Sometimes ice looks clear like liquid water. If the ice looks clear there is very little air trapped between the ice crystals. When it is white there is air in the ice. Snow is white because there is a lot of air trapped between the ice crystals in each snowflake.

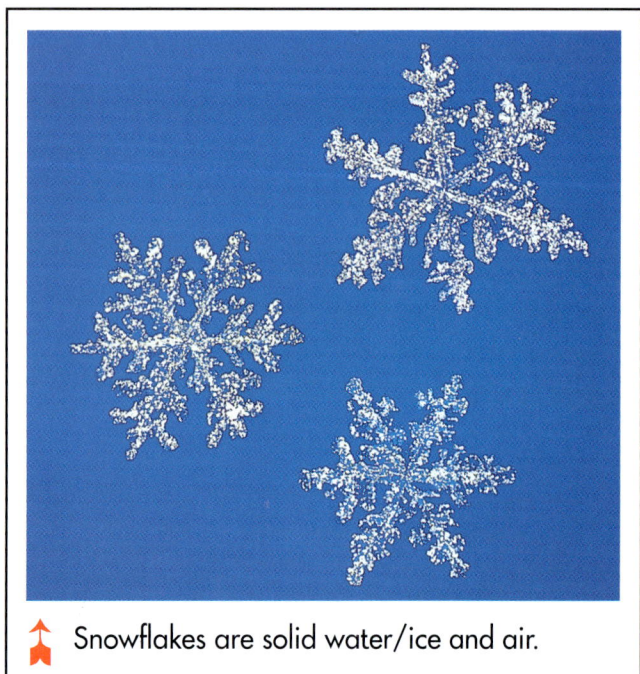

Snowflakes are solid water/ice and air.

Ice and molecules

Ice can float on water because ice is less dense than water. This is because the molecules in water move further away from each other when water becomes ice. This is why water expands when it freezes.

In ice the molecules are further away from each other than in water but they cannot move easily. This is why ice keeps its shape.

The surface of ice

The surface of ice on a pavement is slippery because it melts when your feet press on it. A thin layer of water forms on the bottom of your shoes when they press on the ice. This stops your shoes gripping so you slide around on the ice.

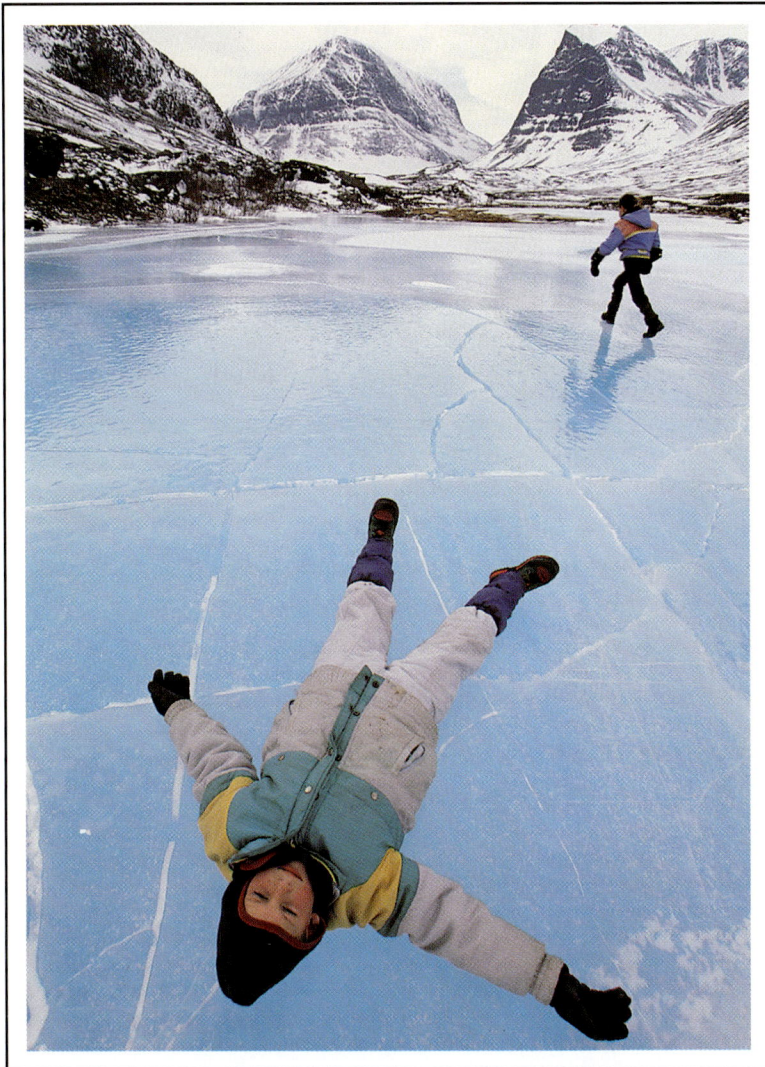

The surface of ice is a very busy place. On the surface some molecules will be melting. Some molecules might even shoot away from the surface as water vapour. Even surface snow in the Arctic can become water vapour.

15

8 Water as a liquid – water

Most water on this Earth is liquid. Liquid water does not keep one shape. Liquids are wet.

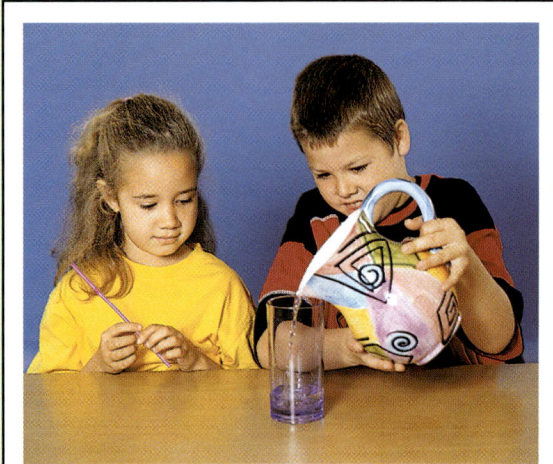

⬆ Liquid water can be poured into any shape. It only stays that shape because the container stops it from running downwards and into the ground.

⬆ Water flows downwards.

Liquid water flows. It flows downhill in rivers and streams. The force of gravity makes water go downwards and into the ground. However, water can be made to flow upwards. Plants make water flow upwards. Water will flow up very thin tubes. Plants have roots and stems with very thin tubes inside them. Water flows up these tubes into the plant.

Liquid water feels wet because when we touch it a very thin layer of water sticks to our skin. This water evaporates making our skin feel cooler.

Liquid water and molecules

In liquid water the molecules can move easily. This is why water does not keep its shape. The molecules slide around each other making the water flow. As water gets warmer the molecules move more quickly around each other. As the water gets cooler they move more slowly.

The surface of water

Tiny insects called pond skaters can walk on liquid water. These insects can walk on the surface of the water because surface tension stops them sinking into the water. Surface tension is a force. Surface tension pulls on the surface of the water, making a thin, stretchy 'skin' on the top.

⬆ Pond skaters are so light they can walk on the 'skin' on the top of the water.

9 Water as a gas –
water vapour

Water vapour is a gas. When a puddle dries up the water escapes into the air in tiny droplets called water vapour. The droplets are too small to see.

Steam is water vapour. Steam is invisible. If you look carefully at a boiling kettle, you will see that there is a place just above the spout where the air looks clear. This is steam. As the steam rises into the air it cools and becomes a mass of tiny water drops. These make clouds. These clouds are a mixture of steam, air and tiny drops of liquid water.

There is always water vapour in the air around us. We cannot usually see the water in the air, but if there is a lot of water vapour in the air around us the air feels moist. The air in the rainforests near the Equator feels moist. If there is very little water vapour in the air it feels dry. The air in the desert feels dry.

The amount of water in the air can be measured. It is called the humidity. Rainforests have high humidity because the warm air can hold a lot of water vapour. The warmer the air the more water vapour it can hold.

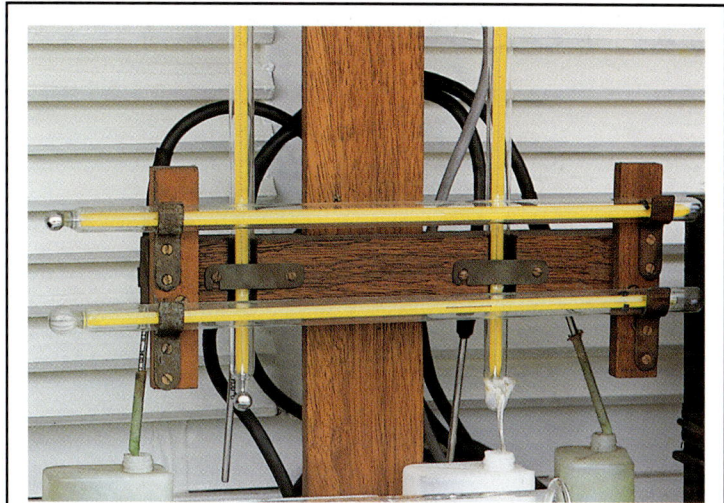
A hygrometer measures humidity.

Water vapour and molecules

The molecules in a gas or vapour move very quickly, shooting off in all directions. In a gas the molecules are not linked together. We cannot see single molecules, this is why gases are hard to see. It is easy to see a handful of flour but almost impossible to see a single speck of flour. Just like the flour, when molecules are all together they can be easy to see but when they are not linked together they are hard to see.

Steam condenses

Steam

Boiling water

Steam can be seen once it condenses.

19

10 The water cycle

The warm water vapour meets cold air. This is because the air higher in the sky is much cooler.

The water vapour rises up into the sky with the warm air. Drier air takes its place. When it is windy, the warm air, full of water vapour, is moved quickly away from the water.

The sun warms water. Some of the warm water turns into water vapour.

We call the way that water moves around the Earth the water cycle. Water moves round and round the Earth like the wheels on a bike moving round and round. When something moves round and round we call it a cycle.

When the water vapour cools it turns back into drops of water. This change from water vapour back to water is called condensation.

The drops of water form clouds. When the clouds become heavy with lots of raindrops, it rains. When it is very cold the water in the clouds falls as snow.

How the water moves in the water cycle

The rain falls into the seas, lakes and rivers and onto the land. Most of the rain flows downhill towards the sea in rivers and streams. Some rain soaks into the land and flows towards the sea underground.

The sun shines and the fallen rainwater changes into water vapour again. The cycle continues forever and ever.

11 Summary

Water is always moving around the Earth. At this very minute some of the water on Earth is changing from water to water vapour and from water vapour to water. Ice will be turning to water and water will be turning to ice. Water is remarkable because it can change from one form to another and back again. When most things are heated they change. When an egg is heated it turns solid. We cannot make the egg runny again. When the egg is cooled it does not melt, it stays solid.

Water is unusual. It can change forms again and again without becoming permanently a gas, a solid or a liquid.

High cloud

Snow

Low cloud

Mountain

Ice

Lake

Glossary

Cloud	A cloud is made up of a mass of tiny water droplets light enough to float in the air.
Condensation	Condensation is the change from a vapour into a liquid.
Evaporation	Evaporation is the change from a liquid to a vapour.
Freeze	When a liquid freezes it becomes solid. Water freezes when it becomes ice.
Frost	Frost is frozen dew or water vapour. Frost forms on cold objects.
Gas	A gas is very light and cannot usually be seen. Air is made of gases. Water vapour is water as a gas.
Gravity	Gravity is a force which pulls objects down to Earth. If there were no gravity everything would float away into space.
Liquid	A liquid is something that can be poured. Liquids can easily change their shape. Water, milk and oil are liquids.
Melt	When a solid melts it becomes liquid. When ice melts it becomes water.
Molecules	Molecules are the minute building blocks used to make all solids, liquids and gases. Molecules are too small for us to see without help.
Solid	A solid cannot change shape. Solids are usually hard. Ice, wood and metal are solid.
Temperature	Temperature is a measure of how hot or cold something is. It is usually measured in degrees Celsius (°C).
Thermometer	A thermometer is an instrument used to measure temperature.
Vapour	A vapour is an invisible gas in the air. Water becomes vapour when it evaporates.

Further information

Books

Eyewitness Science Guides: How science works by Judith Hann, Dorling Kindersley 1997

Weather: Nature Detective by Anita Ganeri, Franklin Watts 1993

Science in Our World: Weather by Brian Knapp, Earthscape Editions, Atlantic Europe Editions 1990

Index

a b c d e f g h i j k l m n o p q r s t u v w x y z
A B C D E F G H I J K L M N O P Q R S T U V W X Y Z